SHAKESPEARE'S
BOOK OF WISDOM

Advice on Living a Wiser, Happier Life
From William Shakespeare & Friends

Prince Hamlet meets Yorick. Again.

SHAKESPEARE'S
BOOK OF WISDOM

Advice on Living a Wiser, Happier Life
From William Shakespeare & Friends

ROB CRISELL

DEPORTOLA PRESS
Temecula

DEPORTOLA PRESS
Temecula

ISBN: 978-0-692-18673-2

DePortola Press
33780 Linda Rosea Road
Temecula, CA 92592
www.robcrisell.com

For information about custom editions, special sales, and premium and corporate purchases, contact DePortola Press at (951) 551-5338 or robcrisell@yahoo.com, or at the address above.
Third Printing April 2019

Printed in the United States of America

10 9 8 7 6 5 4 3 2 1

www.robcrisell.com

Cover art by Nicholas Ivins
Book design by Charles King (ckmm.com) and Rob Crisell

Contents

❀ ❀ ❀ ❀ ❀ ❀

Prospero and his daughter Miranda. Parenting is hard magic.

For my son Soren, my father Bob,
And all others who hunger for wisdom.

If this be error and upon me proved,
I never writ, nor no man ever loved.

SONNET 116

These fragments I have shored against my ruins.

T.S. Eliot

INTRODUCTION

❖ ❖ ❖ ❖ ❖ ❖

Thy life's a miracle!

KING LEAR, Act 4, Scene 6

I have written this book as a gift for you. It's not the kind of present you can enjoy passively, like a laptop or a new car. Reaping a harvest from it requires patience, hard work, passion, and dedication. But if you are able to incorporate its wisdom into your life, it will make you happier than anything else I could give you.

I'm not the source of this book's wisdom. "A wise man will hear, and will increase learning," writes the author of Proverbs. I've increased my learning mostly by paying heed to William Shakespeare, whose works have meant so much to me and millions of others over the centuries. While he may not have been a philosopher or a theologian, Shakespeare and his remarkable characters ("free artists of themselves," in Hegel's words) have much to say on the subject of wise and happy living. In fact, I think that if one studied *only* the collected works, one would have all the tools one needs for a good life. Just to be on the safe side, though, I've enlisted the help of a few dozen other poets, philosophers, saints, and sinners in the same wisdom tradition as the Bard. These are folks with whom Shakespeare might have liked to drink a cup of ale — or at least *I* would have.

I'm not the best practitioner of this book's wisdom. Portia in the *Merchant of Venice* speaks for me when she says that it's "easier to teach twenty what were good to be done, than be one of the twenty to follow mine own teaching." I've written this book mostly to help me understand and articulate my own philosophy of life and only secondarily to persuade you of its

William Shakespeare — poet, philosopher, snappy dresser.

truth. In this, I imitate Michel de Montaigne, who says of his *Essays*: "This book is not my teaching but my study." In other words, we're in this together.

Finally, I'm keenly aware that I'm just another in a long list of parents from Polonius to Scott Fitzgerald to George Patton who felt compelled to write down their advice to their children. The author of Ecclesiastes is unimpressed with such efforts: "Of making many books there is no end, and much study is wearisome to the flesh. Let us hear the conclusion of the whole matter: Fear God and keep his commandments, for this is man's all."

I suppose he's right. But it's human nature to try to make old truths new again, so it's my turn to add one more book to the pile.

Thomas Sowell observes that every new generation is an "invasion of civilization by little barbarians, who must be civilized before it is too late." While you may have been given extraordinary gifts of intelligence, grace, patience, and artistic ability, you're still one of Sowell's barbarians compared to the person you'll be in five, ten, and twenty years. Resist the complacency of youth. The world will prosper only if you and others work to embody the eternal truths of this book in your lives. Otherwise, little barbarians will grow up to be big barbarians and society will be the worse off for it.

If you believe that there is more to existence than materialism without spirit, knowledge without prudence, and power without love, keep the flickering candle of wisdom burning. Test this book's advice, make it your own, and pass it on.

— ROB CRISELL
April 2019

1. GIVE SO THAT YOU CAN RECEIVE.

There's none can truly say he gives, if he receives.

TIMON OF ATHENS, Act 1, Scene 2

IN OTHER WORDS . . .

Generosity is its own reward.

MONEY IS THE LIFEBLOOD OF EVEN THE MOST CHARITABLE organizations. Often the easiest, most efficient way to practice charity is to give money to a favorite non-profit, a church, friends, family, or strangers. However, when it comes to growing in wisdom, it is the giving of time and talent that matters most. This kind of giving requires much more effort than writing a check, since time is more precious than money. Money donated to great causes helps those causes, but it doesn't directly help us. But when we give our time, we give ourselves. The time we spend in helping others is never wasted—it is redeemed. That is the paradox of giving: As much as we give to others, we receive even more.

He who sows sparingly will also reap sparingly,
and he who sows bountifully will also reap bountifully.

2 CORINTHIANS 9:6

2. USE YOUR ARTISTIC TALENTS
TO BRING JOY TO OTHERS.

Preposterous ass, that never read so far
To know the cause why music was ordain'd!
Was it not to refresh the mind of man
After his studies or his usual pain?

THE TAMING OF THE SHREW, Act 3, Scene 1

IN OTHER WORDS . . .

Music was created to make people happy.

LET US TRY TO USE OUR ARTISTIC TALENTS TO BRING OTHERS JOY. When we engage our artistic sides, we tap into a phenomenon infinitely greater than ourselves — greater even than a movement or epoch. Although we may not think of ourselves as strong artists, even our limited abilities are capable of bringing happiness and meaning to other people. They allow us the opportunity and privilege to share our gifts and talents. In the end, that might be art's highest purpose. As you fall more deeply in love with your art, allow it to inspire you to share that love with others.

> *Art enables us to find ourselves*
> *and lose ourselves at the same time.*
>
> THOMAS MERTON

3. DON'T LET YOUR ANGER
CONTROL YOU.

Anger's my meat; I sup upon myself,
And so shall starve with feeding.

CORIOLANUS, Act 4, Scene 2

IN OTHER WORDS . . .

Those who try to feed on their anger
famish their own souls.

ANGER — NOT LUST, GREED, SADNESS, JOY, OR LOVE — PRODUCES the strongest emotions most quickly in human beings. These days, no emotion seems to be more prevalent in our society. We get angry at others. We get angry at ourselves. We rage against the government, political opponents, God, family, friends, and strangers. Resentment, fear, ignorance, and hate add to the polluted atmosphere of anger that permeates our culture.

None of this anger is helpful. When we succumb to it, we give ourselves over to powerful forces that harm us and those around us. Anger tends to destroy rather than build up. It burns brightly but leaves ashes in its wake. Sustained wrath and hostility over many years also curdles our spirit and poisons our relationships with others. True, it might be better to be angry than indifferent in the face of injustice and wrongdoing. But after the anger, we should find ways of solving problems through fruitful action and thoughtful communication. Get angry when necessary, but get over it quickly.

Anger dwells only in the bosom of fools.

ALBERT EINSTEIN

4. BE CHEERFUL, EVEN WHEN LIFE IS HARD.

Be cheerful; wipe thine eyes:
Some falls are means the happier to arise.

CYMBELINE, Act 4, Scene 2

IN OTHER WORDS . . .

Cheer up and stop crying. What doesn't kill you
sometimes makes you stronger.

CHEERFULNESS SEEMS TO HAVE LITTLE TO DO WITH WISDOM, but the two are intimately related. When we're friendly and open to others, we demonstrate good character, self-awareness, confidence, and humility. Conversely, when we're callous and angry we show the world that we're too obsessed with our own lives to concern ourselves with those of others. That's why we need to develop a habit of cheerfulness. Don't underestimate the power of a positive attitude. Happiness is contagious. "Joy delights in joy," as Sonnet 8 puts it. Or as St. Teresa of Calcutta writes: "Joy is a net of love by which we catch souls."

Of course, anyone can be cheerful when they're comfortable and worry-free. It's much more difficult during times of adversity. "There was never yet philosopher that could endure the toothache patiently," says Leonato in *Much Ado About Nothing*. Wise people remain positive even in the midst of strife. A cheerful mindset will help us endure hard times more patiently.

The most certain sign of wisdom is cheerfulness.

MICHEL DE MONTAIGNE

5. SHOW COMPASSION TO ALL.

Love all, trust a few, do wrong to none.

ALL'S WELL THAT ENDS WELL, Act 1, Scene 1

IN OTHER WORDS . . .

Love everyone, trust a few, and don't hurt anyone.

TOO OFTEN WE FEEL COMPASSION FOR *CATEGORIES* OF people rather than for individuals themselves. We prefer theoretical humans to actual ones. (Others have given up on humanity altogether and mistakenly believe that kindness to animals is all one needs to be a good person, but that's another story.) But it's impossible to be kind to "paper people." Abstract concern for causes or groups — whether it's the poor, the oppressed, refugees, minorities, or the handicapped — gives us short bursts of self-satisfaction and makes us feel that our opinions and emotions are the same as actions. Real kindness, however, means loving real people: the waiter serving us food, the annoying person at school or work, the elderly woman next to us on an airplane. These people fall into the category that should matter to us the most — human beings in our vicinity.

Use your interactions with others to understand and relate to them. If you treat people with respect and love, they'll be more likely to respond in kind. But even if they don't, do it anyway because it's good for you.

> *Be kind, for everyone you meet*
> *is fighting a hard battle.*
>
> PLATO

6. NEVER STOP LEARNING.

Study is like the heaven's glorious sun
That will not be deep-searched with saucy looks:
Small have continual plodders ever won
Save base authority from others' books.

LOVE'S LABOR'S LOST, Act 1, Scene 1

IN OTHER WORDS . . .

Learning is too vast to be contained
entirely in books. Reading only takes you so far.

WE SHOULD NEVER ASSUME THAT EDUCATION WILL INCREASE our wisdom or good sense. It probably won't. "Book learning" makes us smarter but not always wiser. It might even turn us into "more clever devils," as C. S. Lewis puts it. Yet students of history know how crucial education is when it comes to sustaining a free, just, and prosperous society. These days, educators seem more willing than ever to exchange educational goals of truth, beauty, reason, and wisdom for political goals of tolerance, equality, and diversity. This means that young people are increasingly unprepared to be wise leaders. They often no longer receive the kind of education necessary to maintain a properly functioning democracy.

That's why it's important to resist the urge to embrace what is new and different simply because certain self-appointed intellectual gatekeepers have blessed it. Sort out useful information from harmful indoctrination and make up your own mind. And never stop learning.

Education begins the gentleman, but reading, good company and reflection must finish him.

JOHN LOCKE

7. STRIVE FOR EQUALITY, BUT NOT AT THE EXPENSE OF LIBERTY.

Let his arms alone;
They were not born for bondage.

CYMBELINE, Act 5, Scene 5

IN OTHER WORDS...

Don't bind his arms; he's a free man.

BEWARE OF THOSE WHO AGITATE FOR EQUALITY OF *RESULTS* rather than equality of *opportunity*. The latter is beneficial and achievable. The former comes only at dire social and economic costs and is ultimately illusory.

Everyone is born with unequal advantages with regard to genetics, race, income, family structure, nationality, gender, wealth, intelligence, and so on. This leads some to believe that equal opportunity is a mirage. They claim that we need godlike arbiters (usually within government) to redistribute advantages across society. Such efforts might be well-intentioned, but when carried to their logical end, they make everyone equally ignorant, impoverished, and even enslaved. Strict social equality is enforceable only at the point of a gun. By contrast, equality of opportunity requires only liberty. If we err on the side of liberty and freedom, we will have more prosperity, more happiness, and more equality for more people.

Exercising liberty, however, doesn't mean we can or should do anything we want. Without wisdom, liberty leads to anarchy and totalitarianism. "What is liberty without wisdom and without virtue?" writes Edmund Burke. "It is the greatest of all possible evils." Or as Luciana puts it in *Comedy of Errors*: "Headstrong liberty is lashed with woe." If we cherish liberty, we must defend virtue and wisdom.

There is all the difference in the world between treating people equally and attempting to make *them equal.*

FRIEDRICH HAYEK

8. DON'T MAKE EXCUSES.

This is the excellent foppery of the world, that when we are sick in fortune — often the surfeit of our own behavior — we make guilty of our disasters the sun, the moon, and stars; as if we were villains on necessity; fools by heavenly compulsion.

KING LEAR, Act 1, Scene 2

IN OTHER WORDS...

How ridiculous it is for us to blame our problems — which are usually caused by our own bad decisions — on the stars and planets; as if we were predestined to be villains.

LIFE ISN'T FAIR. WE HAVE ALL BEEN TREATED UNJUSTLY. We've been overlooked for our hard work. We've been blamed for the mistakes of others. As a result, we've grumbled and complained to anyone who would listen. Guess what? No one wants to hear our excuses, regardless of how reasonable they might be. Our self-justifications and excuses only turn us into victims — passive targets of life's slings and arrows. As the evil (yet perceptive) Edmund observes in *King Lear*: "An admirable evasion of whoremaster man, to lay his goatish disposition on the charge of a star." These days, we might not blame stars for our problems, but blaming society, fate or bad luck is almost as harmful.

Don't make excuses. Instead, make peace with the fact that life is often difficult and unfair. Seize responsibility for your own life. Only when you do can you become the hero of the autobiographical movie blockbuster that is your life. After all, if you don't take the role, no one else will.

Never complain; never explain.

BENJAMIN DISRAELI

9. BE REASONABLE BY BEING A PERSON OF FAITH.

It is required you do awake your faith.

THE WINTER'S TALE, Act 5, Scene 3

IN OTHER WORDS . . .

You need faith to experience all that life has to offer.

RELIGIOUS BELIEF IS BEYOND OUR REASON, BUT IT IS NOT necessarily unreasonable. Humans require purpose, hope, and love to be happy. None of these things is rooted firmly in reason. We take leaps of faith when we love someone, when we act kindly with no expectation of reward, or when we forgive in the face of animosity. If we reduce human existence to the physical plane, we blind ourselves to what matters most. Ultimately, only faith helps give us the mindset necessary for a happy life. Believing in the unseen God encourages us to view the world through the eyes of faith. When we do this, we find meaning where there was only nihilism; love where there was only will to power; order where there was only chaos; joy where there was only pleasure. We see the soul inside the skin. With Hamlet, we learn that there are "more things in heaven and earth than are dreamt of in our philosophy."

*The supreme function of reason is to show us
that some things are beyond reason.*

BLAISE PASCAL

10. STRIVE FOR EXCELLENCE, NOT FAME.

Glory is like a circle in the water,
Which never ceaseth to enlarge itself
Till by broad spreading it disperse to nought.

HENRY VI, PART I, Act 1, Scene 2

IN OTHER WORDS . . .

Fame is like the ripples created after a stone is thrown
into a pond. It lasts only as long as the ripples.

PEOPLE WHO CLAIM THAT THEY'VE NEVER WANTED TO BE famous are probably not telling the truth. Fame has a nearly irresistible allure for most of us. It takes hold of everyone, if only for a little while. This is understandable since the desire for fame is a longing for love or immortality or both. Such feelings are hardwired in human beings.

There is a world of difference, however, between idly wishing to be famous and making the sacrifices necessary to achieve it. Fame makes few happy and many unhappy. It's like a drug that provides brief moments of euphoria, followed by long periods of anxiety, insecurity, self-loathing, jealousy, or depression. A life dominated by a quest for fame is unfulfilling and empty. It can even be torture.

Such steep costs aren't worth the benefits. Pursue excellence in your profession or avocation with passionate determination as a good unto itself. Or pursue it to let "your light shine before others, so that they may see your good works and give glory to your Father in heaven," as the author of Matthew writes. But if you do it for money or fame, you'll be disappointed.

> *Worldly fame is but a breath of wind that blows*
> *now this way, and now that, and changes name*
> *as it changes direction.*
>
> DANTE ALIGHIERI

11. REMEMBER HOW MUCH YOU OWE YOUR FAMILY.

How sharper than a serpent's tooth it is
To have a thankless child.

KING LEAR, Act 1, Scene 4

IN OTHER WORDS . . .

It is easier to endure a snake bite than an ungrateful child.

MANY OF THE WORLD'S PROBLEMS CAN BE TRACED BACK TO bad parenting and broken families. Perhaps the greatest gift that parents can give their children is a stable, reasonably happy family life. The importance of such a gift extends far into the future. Family is the foundation not only of our lives but also of the lives of our children — even our children's children. When we pray for a happy life, we should pray for a strong marriage and a loving family. When we give God thanks, we should thank him for two parents who love each other as much as they love us. But even if our parents don't love each other anymore, they made us who we are more than anything else in our lives. Be sure that the person you marry understands how high the stakes are.

As the family goes, so goes the nation
and so goes the whole world in which we live.

JOHN PAUL II

12. REALIZE THAT GOOD FRIENDS ARE RARE.

Those friends thou hast, and their adoption tried,
Grapple them unto thy soul with hoops of steel.

HAMLET, Act 1, Scene 3

IN OTHER WORDS . . .

Once you have found someone who has proven herself
to be a true friend, don't let that person go.

NEVER UNDERESTIMATE THE VALUE OF A GOOD FRIEND. Friendships in childhood are relatively plentiful. As we get older, our expectations for what constitutes a strong friendship become more complex and demanding. These are the signs of a real friend: good communication; faith in each other; genuine happiness in each other's company; unconditional acceptance; support during failures and successes; unselfish giving of themselves. It's no surprise that these are also the hallmarks of a strong marriage. When you find a true friend — a person with whom you can be your authentic self — cherish him or her. As Samuel Johnson advises, "keep that friendship in constant repair" because such friends are rare and wonderful.

While the relationship we have with our spouse will be the most consequential for us, our close friendships with others deeply enrich our lives. Friends are to life what salt is to food: They aren't necessary for us to live, but our lives are so much better with them. When you find a true friend, don't take them for granted. As Hamlet tells Horatio, wear them in your "heart's core," your "heart of hearts."

> *There is no possession more valuable*
> *than a good and faithful friend.*

SOCRATES

13. TO FIND GENIUS, LOOK FOR PASSION.

Lovers and madmen have such seething brains,
Such shaping fantasies, that apprehend
More than cool reason ever comprehends.

A MIDSUMMER NIGHT'S DREAM, Act 5, Scene 1

IN OTHER WORDS . . .

The imaginations of lunatics and lovers
are more fertile than those of reasonable people.

WE WILL ENCOUNTER MANY PEOPLE THROUGHOUT OUR LIVES who are clever, wise, and even brilliant. But we'll meet only a handful of geniuses. One quality that unites people of genius is that they use their extraordinary gifts in passionate service to others. Without the passion, genius remains sterile, solitary, and stunted. Every person has a spark of genius. To unleash your full potential, draw on your reservoirs of generosity, joy, wisdom, and especially passion. "Nothing great was ever achieved without enthusiasm," writes Ralph Waldo Emerson. Passion for your art, your profession, your faith, and your fellow humans will allow your brilliant ideas to bear fruit.

> *Neither a lofty degree of intelligence nor imagination*
> *nor both together go to the making of genius.*
> *Love, love, love — that is the soul of genius.*
>
> WOLFGANG AMADEUS MOZART

14. DON'T SPEAK UNKINDLY
ABOUT ANYONE.

I will chide no breather in the world but myself, against whom I know most faults.

AS YOU LIKE IT, Act 3, Scene 2

IN OTHER WORDS . . .

I refuse to criticize anyone but myself,
since I'm most aware of my own failings.

WE WOULD ALL BE HAPPIER AND LESS ANXIOUS IF WE resolved never to say anything negative about people behind their backs. Gossip might be universally condemned, but it's also universally popular, especially among people unhappy with their own lives. Those who spread gossip are often motivated by envy, disdain, resentment, and insecurity. Avoid them if you can. Remember that whoever gossips *to* you likely also gossips *about* you. Those who reveal the secrets of others will not keep yours. Surround yourself with people who are loathe to talk badly about others, are honest with themselves, and are slow to cast judgment.

Never say or do anything until you have asked yourself
whether it will be pleasing to God, good for yourself,
and edifying to your neighbor.

ST. IGNATIUS OF LOYOLA

15. Be skeptical of government, even one with good intentions.

O, how wretched is that poor man that hangs on princes' favors!

HENRY VIII, Act 3, Scene 2

IN OTHER WORDS . . .

Pity those who must depend on the government.

SELF-INTEREST MIGHT SOUND LIKE A DIRTY WORD, BUT WHEN it comes to a free-market economy, it's a beautiful thing. It's also vital for human prosperity in a free society. Rational self-interest transforms the survival instinct — for oneself, one's family, or one's tribe — into a powerful engine for social good. That's why it's better to rely on the self-interest of many individuals invested in the success of a free market and acting under the same set of laws than the supposed good intentions of a powerful, all-encompassing government. People are flawed, selfish, and capable of all evil. Since government is made up of people, it will necessarily reflect all their negative characteristics. Therefore, if we hand over most decisions regarding our self-interest to those who govern us, we should expect less freedom and less prosperity as a result.

Don't expect corporations or governments to have good intentions. It's not in their nature. If they produce desirable products and services at a market price, their intentions don't matter. Expect compassion from friends, polite indifference from strangers, and benign self-interest from everyone else.

It is not from the benevolence of the butcher, the brewer, or the baker that we expect our dinner, but from their regard to their own interest.

ADAM SMITH

16. Show your gratitude daily.

I hate ingratitude more in a man
Than lying, vainness, babbling, drunkenness,
Or any taint of vice whose strong corruption
Inhabits our frail blood.

Twelfth Night, Act 3, Scene 4

In Other Words . . .

Ingratitude is the worst of all the vices that plague
sinful humankind.

MAINTAIN A GRATEFUL OUTLOOK ON LIFE. ALWAYS BE THANK-
ful for what you have and who you are. Gratitude is solid evidence
of humility, which is the foundation of all virtues. It's also a
reliable gauge of self-awareness. Grateful people are happy with
much or little. Ungrateful people are unhappy regardless of how
much they have. Be thankful for being placed on Earth at this
moment in history. Be thankful to parents and grandparents
for their love, knowledge, and wisdom. Be thankful for friends,
pastors, teachers, coaches, employers, and others who influence
us most directly. And be sure to show your gratitude in tangible
ways — don't keep it to yourself. Like Sebastian in *Twelfth Night*,
be lavish in your gratitude: "I can no other answer make but
thanks and thanks; and ever thanks!"

Gratitude is not only the greatest of virtues,
but the parent of all the others.

CICERO

17. MAKE UP YOUR MIND TO BE HAPPY.

Our bodies are our gardens, to the which our wills are gardeners.

OTHELLO, Act 1, Scene 3

IN OTHER WORDS . . .

Our body is a garden and our willpower is the gardener.
We are what we sow.

SOME PEOPLE THINK THAT HAPPINESS IS SIMPLY AN emotion — a temporary feeling of contentment that ebbs and flows depending on our fortunes. We're happy when we get a new car, unhappy when that car breaks down. In this view, we're passive recipients of good or ill events that dictate our emotions. But true happiness doesn't come from outside us, it comes from within. Happiness is a *choice*. It isn't an emotion but a frame of mind that we can control through our will. It's like the sun — storm clouds might obscure it from time to time, but it remains as strong and vibrant as ever beneath the gloom.

Some people are rarely happy despite enormous success and good fortune. Others remain generally happy regardless of their situation. Joy can only take root in a fertile soil of gratitude, humility, cheerfulness, and faith. If these virtues grow in our garden, happiness will blossom despite all adverse conditions. Then, in the words of St. Francis de Sales, we can truly "bloom where we are planted."

Most people are about as happy
as they make up their minds to be.

ABRAHAM LINCOLN

18. DON'T RELY ON MATERIAL GOODS FOR YOUR HAPPINESS.

Poor and content is rich, and rich enough,
But riches fineless is as poor as winter
To him that ever fears he shall be poor.

OTHELLO, Act 3, Scene 3

IN OTHER WORDS . . .

If you're poor but happy, you're wealthy enough. But all the
riches in the world aren't enough for someone
who is afraid he's going to lose it all.

ALL THE POSSESSIONS AND ACCOMPLISHMENTS IN THE WORLD will never give us lasting happiness. If we think we'll be happy only when we have fame, riches, love, children, health, friends, or a great career, then we will *never* be happy. However, if we have faith in God and do our best to love our neighbor, we already possess all that we need. By putting first things first, blessings only add to our joy while misfortunes cause us no lasting harm.

You can never get enough of what
you don't need to make you happy.

ERIC HOFFER

19. TO STAY HEALTHY,
USE COMMON SENSE.

Brutus is wise, and, were he not in health,
He would embrace the means to come by it.

JULIUS CAESAR, Act 2, Scene 1

IN OTHER WORDS . . .

Wise people seek remedies when they're sick or worried.

MENTAL WELL-BEING AND PHYSICAL WELL-BEING ARE DIFFERENT sides of the same coin. One without the other is almost useless. What unites them is common sense. Common sense is wisdom's first cousin. It teaches us to moderate our intake of food and drink. It tells us that we need to work, exercise, and play, but that too much of any can be wasteful or even injurious. It teaches us not to pollute our minds with useless or harmful behavior. It instructs us not to worry excessively, to control our emotions, to maintain a positive attitude, to practice good habits, and to act virtuously. Finally, when adversities arrive in the form of injuries, illness, or old age, common sense teaches us to bear them with patience, since these evils visit all of us at some point in our lives. In short, common sense is necessary for living a good life.

Good health and good sense
are two of life's greatest blessings.

PUBILIUS SYRUS

20. STAY PHYSICALLY FIT.

I have of late — but wherefore I know not — lost all my mirth, forgone all custom of exercise.

HAMLET, Act 2, Scene 2

IN OTHER WORDS . . .

Lately, I've been so unhappy that I've stopped exercising.

THERE ARE MANY REASONS TO STAY PHYSICALLY STRONG AND in good shape. The relationship between our body and mind is complex but significant. Our brain doesn't function properly when we allow our body to deteriorate through inactivity or abuse. Too often, however, we find excuses for why being physically fit doesn't matter. We place ourselves in artificial categories that harm us or limit our potential. For instance, if we think of ourselves as intellectuals, introverts, or artists, we might decide that these categories preclude us from joining other "clubs," such as athletes or leaders. But these categories exist only in our minds. Staying fit doesn't mean that we have to adopt the lifestyle or mindset of a stereotypical athlete, any more than being friendly turns us into social butterflies. When we put ourselves in these artificial categories, we risk attracting similarly artificial people while repelling those in search of an authentic person who is confident, self-aware, and well balanced.

Exercise and application produce order in our affairs,
health of body, cheerfulness of mind, and these
make us precious to our friends.

THOMAS JEFFERSON

21. TRUST THAT HISTORY HAS MEANING, BUT DON'T HOPE TO UNRAVEL IT.

What's past is prologue.

THE TEMPEST, Act 2, Scene 1

IN OTHER WORDS . . .

If you study the past, you can
predict the future with some accuracy.

"HISTORY DOESN'T REPEAT ITSELF, BUT IT RHYMES," MARK TWAIN allegedly observed. God is an artist and his masterpiece is an epic poem or a symphony that plays until the end of time. Like many works of genius, history is often inscrutable; we get confused and struggle during challenging or unpleasant movements and acts. Like a complex symphony, there are recurring motifs, signatures, and movements. It is continually present because it contains the past yet reaches into the future; it's all the same enduring song. Arnold Toynbee described history as "a vision of God's creation on the move." The study of history is the act of trying to understand the mind of the great Composer-Conductor. We will never be able to comprehend this vision completely, but the attempt is always worth the effort.

> *History is a cyclic poem written by time*
> *upon the memories of man.*

PERCY BYSSHE SHELLEY

22. HOPE WITHOUT EXPECTATION.

A pack of blessings lights upon thy back;
Happiness courts thee in her best array;
But, like a misbehaved and sullen wench,
Thou pout'st upon thy fortune and thy love:
Take heed, take heed, for such die miserable.

ROMEO AND JULIET, Act 3, Scene 3

IN OTHER WORDS . . .

You've been given countless blessings, but you don't
appreciate them. Be careful — such people die in despair.

WE ALL WANT SUCCESS NOW. WE WANT PRAISE NOW. WE WANT an end to our hardships now. But if we hope impatiently, the disappointment we feel when our hopes remain unfulfilled may harden into despair. However, if we wait with patient optimism, we remain firmly on the path of wisdom. In the words of T. S. Eliot, we must learn how "to care and not to care." A patient hope is a grateful hope. While we shouldn't expect the fulfillment of all our hopes, we should try to wait patiently for the arrival of unhoped for joys. As Albert Schweitzer observes, success "is not the key to happiness. Happiness is the key to success." Remain grateful, remain hopeful, and patient.

Hope is patience with the lamp lit.

TERTULLIAN

23. ACCEPT THAT HUMANITY IS FLAWED AND NOT PERFECTIBLE.

Two such opposèd kings encamp them still
In man as well as herbs — grace and rude will;
And where the worser is predominant,
Full soon the canker death eats up that plant.

ROMEO AND JULIET, Act 3, Scene 3

IN OTHER WORDS . . .

Good and evil coexist in humans just as medicine and
poison coexist in certain plants. And when evil
takes over, it destroys a person like a fatal disease.

IN ORDER TO LOVE OUR FELLOW HUMAN BEINGS, WE MUST first understand them. This means coming to terms with the dual nature of the human condition. The beginning of wisdom is a frank acknowledgment that humans are both the "beauty of the world" *and* the "quintessence of dust," in the words of Hamlet. People who deny the coexistence of good and evil in the heart of every person are always baffled, even embittered, by their inability to "solve" such ills as war, poverty, greed, prejudice, and tyranny. They might even flatter themselves that they are the angels who will lead their stubborn comrades to paradise. They grow indignant of and impatient with those who challenge their wrongheaded solutions. But as Montaigne remarks, instead of becoming angels, "they change into beasts; instead of raising themselves, they lower themselves."

This can be avoided if we adopt a realistic, "tragic" view of human nature that acknowledges how flawed we truly are. Such a perspective assumes that peace, prosperity, virtue, and liberty are rare blessings and easily lost unless carefully maintained and safeguarded. Once we recognize human nature for what it is, we can try to love people — including ourselves — for what *we* are.

> *The battle line dividing good and evil*
> *cuts through the heart of every human being.*

ALEXANDER SOLZHENITSYN

24. BE HUMBLE.

I do now remember a saying: 'The fool doth think he is wise, but the wise man knows himself to be a fool.'

AS YOU LIKE IT, Act 5, Scene 1

IN OTHER WORDS . . .

Wise people admit how foolish they are.
Fools mistakenly believe they are wise.

BE HUMBLE OR BE FOOLISH. THOSE ARE THE ONLY OPTIONS. Humility is a sure sign of wisdom. Being humble means consciously and good-naturedly accepting that there are always people who are stronger, faster, kinder, smarter, better-looking, and wiser than us. Indeed, hundreds of millions of people fit this description. Even if you happen to be gifted in one area, chances are you're ignorant or incompetent in many more. This isn't false modesty. It's just a recognition of reality. It is not self-negating, it's self-liberating.

By contrast, arrogant and self-satisfied people possess poor self-awareness and a limited understanding of human nature. They forget the large debts they owe to parents, teachers, coaches, and others who helped them along the way. They often overestimate their intelligence or skills while underestimating those of others. Such people live in a fog of cognitive dissonance when confronted by their deficiencies. They are fools.

Avoid this fate. It has led to the downfall of many great men and women, including King Lear, about whom his daughter Regan correctly remarked: "He hath ever but slenderly known himself." Express your gratitude daily and freely admit your shortcomings, so that you don't get lost in a false sense of being. Take joy in your talents, but stay humble.

Humility is the proper estimate of oneself.

CHARLES SPURGEON

25. Don't confuse knowledge with wisdom.

But man, proud man,
Drest in a little brief authority,
Most ignorant of what he's most assured,
Plays such fantastic tricks before high heaven
As make the angels weep.

Measure for Measure, Act 2, Scene 2

In Other Words . . .

Humans, especially when given a little authority over others,
are at their stupidest just when they think they know it all.
They act so horribly, they make angels weep.

BEING HAPPY, WISE, AND PRODUCTIVE HAS NOTHING TO DO with how knowledgeable we are. We'll meet hundreds of people in our lives who are more intelligent and talented than us. We should appreciate and learn from them if we can and never resent them for their gifts. But true intelligence is much than mere knowledge, even when wielded with expertise and imagination. Smart is good, but wise is better. Knowing when, why, and how to use our intelligence requires courage, discretion, humility, perseverance, and honesty. Only when we apply our knowledge and talents wisely will they reach their full potential.

It takes something more than intelligence
to act intelligently.

FYODOR DOSTOYEVSKY

26. LOVE YOUR COUNTRY.

Be just, and fear not:
Let all the ends thou aim'st at be thy country's,
Thy God's, and truth's.

HENRY VIII, Act 3, Scene 2

IN OTHER WORDS . . .

As long as you are just, don't worry. Everything you do
will be for the good of your country, God, and truth.

FEW VIRTUES TODAY ARE MORE MALIGNED THAN PATRIOTISM. Being a patriot was once regarded as synonymous with being a good citizen. That's not usually the case these days. But love of country is simply the logical progression of Edmund Burke's "little platoons" that make up society: family, neighborhood, town, state. It's natural and good to feel affection for these platoons. In fact, dismissing such love as chauvinism is to deny part of our soul. It ignores human nature and defies common sense.

Love America and defend her against her detractors and enemies. Be proud of her traditions, revere the flag, respect the anthem, and observe her holidays. Treat the men and women who serve our country in the armed forces (especially during time of war) with honor and affection. Not every country is equally great. Not every country is worthy of the love of its citizens. Despite her flaws, America *is* worthy. From our unique founding more than two centuries ago, to the blood spilled to rid our nation of slavery and other nations of dictatorship or poverty, to our history of blending diverse cultures and races into a single republic, to our presence as a beacon of liberty and hope for the entire world, America has earned its patriots. Be one of them.

The liberties of our country, the freedom of our civil Constitution, are worth defending at all hazards. We have received them as a fair inheritance from our worthy ancestors: they purchased them for us with toil and danger and expense of treasure and blood, and transmitted them to us with care and diligence.

SAMUEL ADAMS

27. DEMAND IMPARTIAL BUT IMPERFECT JUSTICE.

O worthy prince, dishonor not your eye
By throwing it on any other object
Till you have heard me in my true complaint
And given me justice, justice, justice, justice!

MEASURE FOR MEASURE, Act 5, Scene 1

IN OTHER WORDS . . .

Don't waste your time pursuing other political goals
until you have fulfilled the cause of justice.

FAIRNESS IS WHAT WE HOPE FOR FROM PRIVATE INDIVIDUALS. Justice is what we should demand from those who police, judge, and govern us. Justice can be described as fair dealing between the governors and the governed. It requires general laws applied equally to everyone, regardless of circumstances of birth or parentage. While we admire fairness, we have less affection for so-called "strict" or "legal" justice, which seems impersonal and rigid. But when politicians, judges, and activists forsake "ordinary" justice in a futile quest for a kind of ideal or "cosmic" justice, the perfect soon becomes the enemy of the good. "Striving to better, oft we mar what's well," as the Duke of Albany says in *King Lear*. The result is often an ad hoc, unjust, even tyrannical, utopianism. In the end, legal justice is the only kind our so-called public servants are capable of administering. Anything more ambitious is also more unjust.

> *If we do not maintain justice,*
> *justice will not maintain us.*

FRANCIS BACON

28. TO BE A LEADER, BE THE KIND OF PERSON YOU WANT TO LEAD.

For forth he goes and visits all his host.
Bids them good morrow with a modest smile.
That every wretch, pining and pale before,
Beholding him, plucks comfort from his looks.

HENRY V, Act 4, Chorus

IN OTHER WORDS . . .

When you lead others, be kind and humble. Those you
lead learn more from your behavior than your words.

SOONER OR LATER, YOU WILL BECOME SOMEONE ELSE'S BOSS. Be ready. Being successful in business or politics is no different from achieving success in any relationship. When you find people you trust, respect, and love, communicate honestly with them and hold them to the same standards to which you hold yourself. Practice what you preach. Model the behavior in yourself that you want others to exhibit. Good people tend to want to follow good people. If you work hard in our chosen field and treat others as you would want to be treated, you will become a leader whether you want to or not.

> *Example is not the main thing in influencing others.*
> *It is the only thing.*
>
> ALBERT SCHWEITZER

29. BELIEVE YOUR LIFE HAS MEANING.

There's a divinity that shapes our ends, rough-hew them how we will.

HAMLET, Act 5, Scene 2

IN OTHER WORDS . . .

God guides us in the right direction,
however often we might mess it up.

WE DESPERATELY WANT LIFE TO MAKE SENSE, BUT IT OFTEN doesn't. We wonder why something bad happened to us or why something good didn't happen. We look back on how we should have done this or shouldn't have done that. Sometimes we think we see glimpses of a divine purpose, but more often we don't. "God has put eternity into man's mind," writes the author of Ecclesiastes. "Yet so that he cannot find out what God has done from the beginning to the end." In other words, the master plan is unclear by design.

Relax. Instead of looking at life as a puzzle to be solved, treat it as a journey or an adventure over which you have only limited control. As Martin Buber writes: "All journeys have secret destinations of which the traveler is unaware." You are part of an amazing story that has a beginning, middle, and end, with a sequel that goes on forever. Don't give up trying to make sense of this great drama, but don't be anxious when you can't. Trust that God has a plan for you even when you don't understand it. And try to enjoy the ride.

> *Life can only be understood backwards,*
> *but it must be lived forwards.*
>
> SØREN KIERKEGAARD

30. MAINTAIN YOUR JOY
IN THE MIDST OF SORROW.

Each substance of a grief hath twenty shadows,
Which shows like grief itself, but is not so;
For sorrow's eye, glazed with blinding tears,
Divides one thing entire to many objects.

RICHARD II, Act 2, Scene 2

IN OTHER WORDS . . .

When we're sad, it feels as if our griefs are multiplied,
even when they're not.

EVERYONE SUFFERS. WE LOSE LOVED ONES, FACE DISAPPOINT-ments, struggle with inner demons, endure physical ailments, and deal with external conflicts. That's life. How we handle these sufferings depends largely on our understanding of life's meaning. Is the purpose of life to avoid unhappiness? Is life worth living only when it is free from pain? Or is suffering a part of life we must experience in order to grow in wisdom?

There's no doubt that suffering can make us wiser. As Scott Peck puts it: "When we avoid the legitimate suffering that results from dealing with problems, we also avoid the growth that problems demand from us." In *Cymbeline,* Imogen says it even more succinctly: "Some griefs are med'cinable." Knowing this, encourage and be patient with those who are suffering, especially if it's *you.* Remember that your life overflows with meaning and goodness, even in the midst of pain, failure, and loss. "Thy life's a miracle!" exclaims Edgar to his suicidal father in *King Lear.* Never let tears blind you to this fundamental reality.

Life is difficult. This is a great truth, one of the greatest truths. It is a great truth because once we truly see this truth, we transcend it. Once we truly know that life is difficult — once we truly understand and accept it — then life is no longer difficult.

M. SCOTT PECK

31. TELL THE TRUTH.

The good I stand on is my truth and honesty:
If they shall fail, I, with mine enemies,
Will triumph o'er my person.

HENRY VIII, Act 5, Scene 1

IN OTHER WORDS . . .

I live by my truth and honesty. If I behave otherwise,
I will join my enemies and rejoice in my own destruction.

ALWAYS TELL THE TRUTH — OR AT LEAST TRY NOT TO LIE. AS A virtue, honesty might be even more fundamental than gratitude or humility. After all, how can we be grateful or humble if we're dishonest with ourselves and others? Lying obliterates the line between our true self and a false self. It destroys relationships among people. Liars live in a state of dread; they forget which lies they've told to which people. Lying also becomes a habit — when we lie to obtain small benefits, we lie to obtain big ones. To maintain healthy relationships with others and live peacefully with yourself, be sure that what you think, say, and do are in harmony with one another. This is the key to living honestly and a prerequisite for a wise and happy life.

Honesty is the first chapter in the book of wisdom.

THOMAS JEFFERSON

32. LOVE AS YOU WOULD BE LOVED.

Love is not love
Which alters when it alteration finds,
Or bends with the remover to remove:
O no! it is an ever-fixèd mark
That looks on tempests and is never shaken.

SONNET 116

IN OTHER WORDS . . .

Love isn't love if it changes when circumstances change.
On the contrary, it's like a lighthouse's beacon that shines
through storms and never wavers.

JESUS COMMANDS US TO LOVE ONE ANOTHER. HE EVEN TELLS US how to do it. "Love one another," he says in the Book of John. "As I have loved you so you must love one another." And how did he love us? He comforted. He healed. He taught. He forgave. Finally, he laid down his life. This is easy to understand, but difficult to imitate. At least it shows us how to discern whether the love we have for a person is authentic. We should ask ourselves *how* we love that person. Is our love dependent on what we can get from them? Is it based primarily on how they make us feel? Can that love be lost in an instant if they say or do the wrong thing? Are we willing to make tremendous sacrifices for them? Is our love kind, patient, and generous? When we understand how others love us and how we love others, we can determine whether that love is profound or superficial.

This is the secret of life: the self lives only by dying,
finds its identity (and its happiness) only by
self-forgetfulness, self-giving, self-sacrifice, and agape love.

PETER KREEFT

33. DON'T IDOLIZE PEOPLE YOU LOVE.

This is the liver-vein, which makes flesh a deity,
A green goose a goddess: pure, pure idolatry.
God amend us, God amend!

LOVE'S LABOR'S LOST, Act 4, Scene 3

IN OTHER WORDS . . .

Idolatry originates in the liver, the mythical seat of love and
violent passion. Those who idolize others turn flesh into a god
and a prostitute into a goddess. God help us!

THERE ARE AT LEAST TWO WAYS OF DEHUMANIZING A PERSON: dismissing them or idolizing them. Many of us would agree that coldly writing off those whom we dislike is wrong. Fewer have reservations about idolizing those we love. In both cases, however, we transform flesh-and-blood individuals into objects of our imagination; we *use* them for our own gain. Whether the object of our worship is a parent, child, lover, artist, intellectual, priest, or politician, when we see them as we *imagine* them to be instead of as they *are*, we harm them and delude ourselves. Human beings should be loved, not worshiped.

Someday you'll have children of your own. You'll love them unconditionally and make great sacrifices for them. But never expect them to fill some existential or God-shaped hole in your life. And don't shield them from corrections, expectations, trials, and responsibilities. Hold them to the same high standards to which you hold yourself. In doing so, you'll benefit them and the whole world.

Everyone should be respected as an individual,
but no one idolized.

ALBERT EINSTEIN

34. BE LOYAL TO YOUR FAMILY, FRIENDS, AND PRINCIPLES.

A jewel in a ten-times-barr'd-up chest
Is a bold spirit in a loyal breast.

RICHARD II, Act 1, Scene 1

IN OTHER WORDS . . .

Loyalty in a friend is as valuable as a priceless jewel
in a well-guarded strongbox.

LOYALTY IS AN UNDERRATED VIRTUE THESE DAYS. IT SOUNDS old-fashioned, even archaic. Some people think only about examples of misplaced loyalty, such as clinging to a bad relationship, an evil cause, or a negative idea. However, whether we call it faithfulness, commitment, or fidelity, loyalty can be a reliable indicator of wisdom. Being loyal to a spouse, a friend, a country, or a worthy principle demonstrates strong character, especially when our allegiance is tested.

If we find ourselves acting disloyally — belittling a family member behind her back or refusing to come to the aid of a friend in need — we should ask ourselves why. Try to recall the original reasons for our faithfulness to that person. Has anything changed? Has our friend ceased being loyal to us? Has a principle to which we once adhered suddenly become invalid? More often, the problem lies not with our friends or our principles but with *ourselves*: our insecurities, jealousies, selfishness, or pride.

Be loyal and trustworthy. Do not befriend anyone
who is lower to yourself in this regard.

CONFUCIUS

35. MARRY WISELY —
AND EARLY IF YOU CAN.

A good leg will fall; a straight back will stoop; a black beard will turn white; a curled pate will grow bald; a fair face will wither; a full eye will wax hollow: but a good heart, Kate, is the sun and the moon.

HENRY V, Act 5, Scene 2

IN OTHER WORDS . . .

Physical beauty in a lover fades as he or she grows old. But a good heart endures as long as the sun and moon.

THE CHOICE OF WHOM TO MARRY IS LIKELY THE MOST SIG-
nificant decision we'll make in our lives. A happy marriage is
among the most important determinants of a fulfilling life. In
marriage, friendship, purpose, and sacrificial love heighten the
sexual experience and invest it with cosmic significance. A strong
marriage serves a purpose similar to that of a strong religious
faith; it allows for infinite growth within a structure that reduces
gross errors in behavior. That's why we should choose our future
spouse wisely and, if possible, *early*. There are advantages to
meeting our future partner when we're young and starting life's
journey together.

But whether you marry early or late, be sure to marry *wisely*.
You marry not only the person your future spouse is when you
meet them, but also the person they will become. Together, you
blend and shape your shared priorities and aspirations. Your wise
and patient influence on your spouse's future self — and theirs on
yours — will determine whether your marriage will be long-lived
and satisfying. And if nothing else, marriage is wisdom-inducing.
As Socrates says: "If you get a good wife, you'll become happy; if
you get a bad one, you'll become a philosopher." Choose wisely.

*In marriage do thou be wise: prefer the person before money,
virtue before beauty, the mind before the body. Then thou hast
a friend, a companion, a second self.*

WILLIAM PENN

36. LIVE OUT THE MEANING OF LIFE THROUGH YOUR ACTIONS.

Action is eloquence.

CORIOLANUS, Act 3, Scene 2

IN OTHER WORDS . . .

Actions speak louder than words.

THE MEANING OF LIFE IS SIMPLE: LOVE GOD AND LOVE YOUR neighbor. In order to live a life of purpose and meaning, we need to put God first and be kind to others. This requires more than good thoughts, it requires good actions. The only way to realize life's meaning is to live it out — to practice what we preach. This is difficult to do. God's plan can be mysterious. People can be awful. Life can be frantic, confusing, and painful. We get caught up in bad habits and addictions. We wonder whether we're living up to our full potential. But it doesn't matter whether we become teachers or bankers, artists or politicians, rich or poor, famous or obscure. Love God and love our neighbor through our actions. Everything else is secondary.

He has shown you, O mortal, what is good. And what does the Lord require of you? To act justly and to love mercy and to walk humbly with your God.

MICAH 6:8

37. BE MERCIFUL TO PEOPLE YOU DON'T LIKE.

The quality of mercy is not strain'd.
It droppeth as the gentle rain from heaven
Upon the place beneath: it is twice blest:
It blesseth him that gives and him that takes.

THE MERCHANT OF VENICE, Act 4, Scene 1

IN OTHER WORDS . . .

No one is forced to show mercy. Mercy should be given freely,
the way rain falls on the ground. It is a double blessing: it
blesses those who give it and those who receive it.

PRACTICING MERCY IS AN ACT OF WISDOM, WHICH IS WHY WISE people love mercy. At its heart, mercy means showing compassion to those who don't deserve it. Being merciful to someone who hasn't earned, or may not even want, our forgiveness magnifies the positive effects of mercy to the benefit of the giver. We shouldn't congratulate ourselves when we're merciful to friends, family, or children. It should be easy to be compassionate to such people. As Jesus says in Luke: "And if you do good to those who do good to you, what benefit is that to you? For even sinners do the same." Being kind to those we love is mostly just common sense. That's not the case with mercy. Mercy isn't always a two-way street. In fact, it isn't even mercy until we show it to those whom we don't like.

> *Where mercy, love, and pity dwell,*
> *there God is dwelling too.*

WILLIAM BLAKE

38. BE MORAL BY ACTING MORALLY.

It is a good divine that follows his own instructions. I can easier teach twenty what were good to be done, than be one of the twenty to follow mine own teaching.

THE MERCHANT OF VENICE, Act 1, Scene 2

IN OTHER WORDS . . .

A pastor is holy if he practices what he preaches.
It's much easier to give good advice than to follow it.

BEING A MORAL PERSON IS ABOUT ACTIONS FIRST, BELIEFS second. Moral action is a necessary attribute of wisdom. Being a good person means *acting* like a good person, regardless of what you *say* you believe. If we want to be moral, we must *act* morally. As the author of Proverbs writes: "Even a child is known by his doings, whether his work be pure, and whether it be right." If we don't put our moral principles into action in our daily lives, they remain no more than good intentions. It's true that good deeds usually follow from good thoughts. As Jesus puts it in Luke: "For a good tree does not bear bad fruit, nor does a bad tree bear good fruit." Ultimately, though, it's the *doing* that matters.

Let your words teach and your actions speak.

ANTHONY OF PADUA

39. RENEW YOUR SPIRIT IN NATURE.

And this, our life, exempt from public haunt,
Finds tongues in trees, books in the running brooks,
Sermons in stones, and good in everything.

AS YOU LIKE IT, Act 2, Scene 1

IN OTHER WORDS . . .

When we experience nature, it's as if we hear trees speak, read
books in streams, listen to stones deliver sermons, and
find something good in every living thing.

AS MODERN CITIZENS OF THE FIRST WORLD, WE USUALLY CLOSE ourselves off to nature. We've traded the natural world for the manufactured one. We're so consumed by technology and other creature comforts that we pay little attention to earth, air, plants, animals, and water. Weather rarely threatens. Nature no longer fascinates. We live in hermetically sealed boxes where dusk has no meaning and dawn holds no wonder.

We've gained much from modernization, but we've lost much as well. We've lived close to nature for too long to remove ourselves completely from it without negative consequences. If we listen, nature can teach us so much about ourselves. It opens up our minds and humbles us. That's why when we visit the oceans, mountains, deserts, and forests, we are energized and inspired. We remember that we're just one part of God's vast creation, even if we are Hamlet's "paragon of animals."

So when you're depressed or anxious, go to the beach, take a hike in the mountains, explore the desert, or walk in the woods. You'll emerge from the experience wiser and happier.

Nature's peace will flow into you as sunshine flows into trees. The winds will blow their own freshness into you, and the storms their energy, while cares will drop off like autumn leaves.

JOHN MUIR

40. BE PATIENT WITH OTHERS.

I do oppose
My patience to his fury, and am arm'd
To suffer, with a quietness of spirit,
The very tyranny and rage of his.

THE MERCHANT OF VENICE, Act 4, Scene 1

IN OTHER WORDS . . .

I'll be as patient as he is furious.
I'll calmly and quietly endure his cruel rage.

PATIENCE IS "THE COMPANION OF WISDOM" JUST AS IMPATIENCE is wisdom's mortal enemy, writes St. Augustine. Erasmus agrees, adding that patience is prudent because it "recognizes human limitations and does not strive to leap beyond them; it is willing to run with the herd, to overlook faults tolerantly or to share them in a friendly spirit." Patience is a form of mercy and, like mercy, it benefits *us* as much as it benefits others. Those who are patient with the flaws of others tend to be happier and more at peace. They are more compassionate, more merciful, more humble, and generally happier than impatient people. Since wise people know that folly and vanity pervade everything in life, especially human behavior, they're also more self-aware. Slow down, think before you speak, and be as patient with your fellow humans as you would have them be with you. You and the world will be better for it.

The more you know yourself, the more patience
you have for what you see in others.

ERIK ERIKSON

41. DON'T LET THE ACTIONS OF OTHERS DICTATE HOW YOU ACT.

Use every man after his desert, and who shall scape whipping? Use them after your own honor and dignity. The less they deserve, the more merit is in your bounty.

HAMLET, Act 2, Scene 2

IN OTHER WORDS . . .

If you treat others according to their merits, no one would escape punishment. Treat them according to your own honor. The less they deserve, the more your generosity is worth.

JESUS' MOST FAMOUS COMMANDMENT IS ALSO HIS LEAST followed: "Do unto others as you would have them do unto you." For the most part, we do unto others *exactly* as they do unto us. It's human nature to give as good as we get. If people are friendly to us, we tend to be friendly to them. When they treat us poorly, we respond in kind, mirroring their anger, impatience, disrespect, and other negative behaviors. This can feel like justice: an eye for an eye, a tooth for a tooth. As Shylock says, when he justifies cutting out a pound of flesh from his antisemitic enemy: "The villainy you teach me, I will execute." Revenge is sweet.

While such feelings are understandable, they're also self-defeating and sometimes illogical. If we disregard our principles whenever someone makes it difficult to adhere to them, are they really our principles? Why should the bad behavior of others determine how *we* behave? Try to be kind, patient, and generous towards people not because *they* are kind, patient, and generous, but because *you* are. By doing so, you'll set a positive example for others and you'll be happier, too.

Do things for people not because of who they are or what they do in return, but because of who you are.

HAROLD KUSHNER

42. NEVER GIVE UP.

Nor stony tower, nor walls of beaten brass,
Nor airless dungeon, nor strong links of iron,
Can be retentive to the strength of spirit.

JULIUS CAESAR, Act 1, Scene 3

IN OTHER WORDS . . .

Courage and a strong will are capable of
overcoming great obstacles.

ALWAYS TRY HARD. PERSEVERANCE TURNS US INTO PEOPLE WHO know that the battle for success never ends. If we make a habit of persevering, we put ourselves in positions to succeed. Making our best effort in all that we do is a good unto itself. But persevering means making the choice to be someone who always *tries*, not someone who always *wins*. Obviously, all the determination in the world won't keep us from falling short at times. Logically, though, perseverance is the only choice: If we make a habit of quitting, we doom ourselves to failure. Those who are quick to give up never accomplish great things. Instead, be like Lucio in *Measure for Measure*, who says: "I am a kind of burr; I shall stick."

Nothing in this world can take the place of persistence.
Talent will not: nothing is more common than unsuccessful
men with talent. Genius will not. Persistence and
determination alone are omnipotent.

CALVIN COOLIDGE

43. Seek to persuade, not to win.

Beauty itself doth of itself persuade
The eyes of men without an orator.

Rape of Lucrece

In Other Words . . .

Real beauty doesn't require an interpreter.
It is self-evidently true and instantly persuasive.

IT IS NEARLY IMPOSSIBLE TO CHANGE THE MINDS OF MOST people when it comes to religion, politics, and other contentious subjects. By the time we're adults, our opinions are very nearly fixed. Our self-definition and self-worth are often inextricably bound up in them; we're emotionally, even existentially, invested. As a result, rhetorical brilliance, trickery, overwhelming data, or bullying will rarely convince our ideological opponents to agree with us, follow us, or love us. In fact, usually when we try to win with such methods, we've already lost.

Persuasion requires a different approach. If we want to persuade, we must present our views humbly while showing genuine sympathy and respect for the views of others. The key lies in Jesus' words in the Book of Mark: "Whoever wishes to become great among you shall be your servant." If we happen to convince someone of a truth that utterly changes his life, it's probably not because of the cleverness of our arguments or the enormity of our intellect. It's because that person was persuaded (typically over time) by our personality, integrity, or authority.

> *Character may almost be called the most*
> *effective means of persuasion.*

ARISTOTLE

44. Be polite.

Ungracious wretch,
Fit for the mountains and the barbarous caves,
Where manners ne'er were preached!
Out of my sight! Rudesby, be gone!

Twelfth Night, Act 4, Scene 1

In Other Words . . .

Rude people are better off living in the wilderness than
among civilized human beings.

WE SHOULD TRY TO BE COURTEOUS TO EVERYONE AND considerate of their needs and feelings. Thomas Macaulay defines politeness as "benevolence in small things." Being polite is one of the costs of living in a civilized society, but it's not an expensive one. Open doors. Say "please" and "thank you." Look people in the eye, don't interrupt, don't condescend, greet strangers cheerfully, don't always insist on your own way, don't gossip, don't brag, respect people with whom you disagree — and don't stop being polite when it's inconvenient. Politeness keeps interactions among strangers civil. It softens encounters among friends and foes alike. It conveys humility and gratitude while maintaining self-respect.

These days, politeness has plenty of enemies. Some claim that it smacks of a master-servant relationship and is therefore oppressive. Others argue that politeness is dishonest and hypocritical; that one should speak one's mind in every situation, disrespect those who disagree with them, curse in public, dispense with honorifics like "Mrs." and "Dr.", and speak bluntly (even rudely) to teachers, preachers, and those in positions of authority. But politeness has nothing to do with subservience or indifference, nor is it a subtle form of dishonesty. It simply acknowledges the value of respect and kindness in our dealings with others. Its ultimate purpose is to preserve human dignity.

Politeness is the result of good sense and good nature.

OLIVER GOLDSMITH

45. When discussing politics, seek clarity, not agreement.

That which combined us was most great, and let not
A leaner action rend us. What's amiss,
May it be gently heard.
Touch you the sourest points with sweetest terms,
Nor curstness grow to the matter.

ANTONY AND CLEOPATRA, Act 2, Scene 2

In Other Words . . .

Since we have so much in common, don't let our petty
differences tear us apart. Listen patiently. Discuss the most
contentious issues most calmly and don't lose your temper.

THERE EXISTS A PIOUS AND PASSIONATE FANATICISM IN POLITICS just as there does in religion. You'll have many frustrating and fiery political arguments in your lifetime. These arguments are usually unresolvable because of a "conflict of visions" at their root. Visions are made up of our intuitive feelings and beliefs about human nature. Thomas Sowell calls them the "constrained" (or "tragic") vision and the "unconstrained" (or "utopian") vision. They often predetermine the outcome of debates on issues as diverse as patriotism, sexuality, race, wealth, the role of government, economics, religion, taxes, war, and justice.

When it comes to such visions, emotion and intuition — not facts — rule the day. As Jonathan Haidt writes: "Moral reasons are the tail wagged by the intuitive dog." This is true even when we believe that our opinions are based solely on facts and objective reasoning. That is why we should be patient with our political and philosophical opponents, striving for mutual understanding and tolerance, not agreement. Empathy is not endorsement. Learn to disagree politely, maintaining respect for your opponents and their right to their own opinions.

And if you can help it, never let politics spoil a good friendship.

At the foundation of moral thinking lie beliefs in statements the truth of which no further reason can be given.

ALASDAIR MacINTYRE

46. PRAY AND BE OPEN TO GOD'S INFLUENCE IN YOUR LIFE.

God shall be my hope,
My stay, my guide and lantern to my feet.

HENRY VI, PART II, Act 2, Scene 3

IN OTHER WORDS . . .

God is my hope, my help, my guide,
and the light unto my path.

PRAYER IS A PROFOUND MYSTERY, WHICH IS HOW MATTERS OF faith should be. "Wisdom and deep intelligence require an honest appreciation of mystery," writes St. Thomas More. The essential mystery of faith is believing that God hears our prayers and desires a relationship with us. Praying acknowledges this relationship. "You have made us for yourself, O Lord," writes St. Augustine. "And our hearts are restless until they find their rest in you." We pray the way an infant cries for its mother, who knows what her child wants before it asks. Humans are at an infinitely greater remove from God than is an infant from its mother. Fortunately, God's love for us is also infinitely greater.

But just as a good parent doesn't spoil her child, God doesn't answer *all* our prayers. That's a good thing. As Menecrates puts it in *Antony and Cleopatra*: "We, ignorant of ourselves, beg often our own harms, which the wise powers deny us for our good." Strive to be grateful and humble before God, and let your prayers go where they will.

Thanksgiving has wings and goes where it must go.
Your prayer knows much more about it than you do.

VICTOR HUGO

47. BE A PERSON OF CHARACTER.

Life every man holds dear; but the dear man
Holds honor far more precious-dear than life.

TROILUS AND CRESSIDA, Act 5, Scene 3

IN OTHER WORDS . . .

Everyone places a high value on life. But a truly good
person values his character even more highly than his life.

BE A PERSON OF CHARACTER BY HOLDING FAST TO WISE PRIN-
ciples such as fairness, honesty, dependability, self-control, and
selflessness. Character is destiny. It determines the kind of person we'll be and the kind of life we'll live. Unlike destiny, however, we have control over our character. Once we identify those
principles by which we hope to live, we need to make them habits.
Then we must try to hold ourselves to those high standards even
when they are inconvenient. If we hope to be good and happy
people, we need to understand that the latter is possible only if
we become the former. Make the development and maintenance
of your character a lifelong mission.

Our character is basically a composite of our habits.
Because they are consistent, often unconscious patterns,
they constantly, daily, express our character.

STEPHEN COVEY

48. READ THE CLASSICS TO GUARD AGAINST NARROW-MINDEDNESS.

My library was dukedom large enough.

THE TEMPEST, Act 1, Scene 2

IN OTHER WORDS . . .

My library was all the kingdom I required.

GREAT LITERATURE IS A SOURCE OF GREAT WISDOM. READING the classics is like opening a portal to the past. It allows us to commune with those who lived before us. It offers us glimpses into the immense treasure trove of wisdom, art, and knowledge of centuries of writers, artists, and thinkers. It keeps us humble by reminding us that there are no new ideas, only new ways of expressing old ones. If we don't read great books, our world-view can easily become a barren landscape occupied only by the opinions of friends, family, teachers, and popular culture. By reading the classics, we develop an appreciation for the width and breadth of humanity and our place in it. "The deepest motive for reading has to be the quest for wisdom," writes Harold Bloom. When we read for wisdom, we become like one of "God's spies" among humankind — as King Lear says — and "take upon us the mystery of things."

*The failure to read good books both enfeebles the vision
and strengthens our most fatal tendency —
the belief that the here and now is all there is.*

ALLAN BLOOM

49. FIND REASONS TO LAUGH.

What is love? 'tis not hereafter;
Present mirth hath present laughter.
What's to come is still unsure.
Youth's a stuff will not endure.

TWELFTH NIGHT, Act 2, Scene 3

IN OTHER WORDS . . .

Love is happening right now. If you feel joy, laugh.
The future is unsure and you won't be young forever.

A SENSE OF HUMOR IS POWERFUL EVIDENCE OF WISDOM. IT shows the world that we don't take ourselves too seriously (humility), that we enjoy making others happy (compassion), and that we aren't afraid of either life or death (courage). It implies a quick mind, a joyful heart, as well as a generous spirit. Humor can even make us feel better, physically and mentally. As the author of Proverbs writes: "A merry heart does good like a medicine."

Like any virtue, however, even a sense of humor can become an evil. There are those who will do anything for a laugh, either because they crave attention or they want to practice their cruelty under the false flag of humor. Avoid such people. But a good sense of humor is almost always a sign of light, not darkness. As Oscar Wilde notes: "Life is much too important to be taken seriously." Laugh often and do your best to help others see the humorous side of life.

*Wit and playfulness represent a desperately serious
transcendence of evil. Humor is both a form of wisdom
and a means of survival.*

TOM ROBBINS

50. TRY YOUR BEST.

If we should fail, we fail.
But screw your courage to the sticking place,
And we'll not fail!

MACBETH, Act 1, Scene 7

IN OTHER WORDS . . .

If we fail, so be it. But be brave and we won't fail.

IT IS OFTEN HARD TO FIND THE COURAGE TO TAKE RISKS. WE think that if we don't try, we can't fail. Since we hate failure, we sometimes decide not to try at all. But *not* trying is a far more insidious type of failure. It leads to self-doubt, regret, even depression. As Mark Twain writes: "Twenty years from now you will be more disappointed by the things that you *didn't* do than by the ones you *did* do." A long succession of failures and triumphs is evidence of a life well-lived. Be brave, take risks, and try your best. And when you fail, brush yourself off and try again.

> *Success is not final, failure is not fatal:*
> *it is the courage to continue that counts.*
>
> WINSTON CHURCHILL

51. Understand first, judge last.

The web of our life is of a mingled yarn, good and ill together: our virtues would be proud, if our faults whipped them not; and our crimes would despair, if they were not cherished by our virtues.

All's Well That Ends Well, Act 4, Scene 3

In Other Words . . .

Our life is like a piece of yarn woven from our good and evil deeds: We'd be arrogant if we didn't recall our vices; we'd despair if we didn't recall our virtues.

HOW DIFFICULT IT IS TO LOVE OUR FELLOW HUMANS! HOW easy it is to judge them! It's hard for us to relate to others in sympathy and love without weighing their shortcomings against their virtues. There exists in our human nature an innate need to categorize, hierarchize, exclude, and condemn. But loving others requires that we first try to understand them. Mockery, disdain, hatred, and even pity don't require such understanding. In fact, often the less we know about someone, the more unsympathetic our view is of that person.

Ultimately, this kind of judging — which is actually "condemning" — hurts *us* more than those whom we judge. Judging is a species of self-comparison; it harms us regardless of whether we compare ourselves favorably or unfavorably. As King Henry says in *Henry VI*: "Forbear to judge, for we are sinners all." Instead, let's make an effort to understand our fellow humans so that we can gradually replace our reflex to judge with an instinct to empathize.

I have striven not to laugh at human actions,
not to weep at them, not to hate them,
but to understand them.

BARUCH SPINOZA

52. Love wisdom more than money.

All that glitters is not gold;
Often have you heard that told:
Many a man his life hath sold
But my outside to behold:
Gilded tombs do worms enfold.

The Merchant of Venice, Act 2, Scene 7

In Other Words . . .

Not all that glitters is gold. People sell their souls for
gorgeous things, but even gold-plated tombs hide maggots.

PEOPLE FREQUENTLY ENLIST JESUS WHEN THEY WANT TO denounce the wealthy. Christ has harsh words for those who put the pursuit of wealth ahead of God's will, since the love of money is fruitless, while the love of God produces everything necessary for a happy life. But the Bible never calls money itself the root of all evil. Instead, it says that *love* of money is the problem. The distinction is important. Most people don't love money for its own sake. Rather, they are grateful for what it can provide their families and their communities: freedom from poverty, increased opportunities, less anxiety, more prosperity. God didn't want us to disdain these blessings, let alone hate them. But if we pursue wealth for its own sake, we gain neither wealth nor lasting satisfaction. Love God, love your neighbor, but don't love *things*.

> *It is not the creation of wealth that is wrong,*
> *but the love of money for its own sake.*
>
> MARGARET THATCHER

53. PUT YOUR LIFE AND DEATH IN PERSPECTIVE.

Cowards die many times before their deaths.
The valiant never taste of death but once.

JULIUS CAESAR, Act 2, Scene 2

IN OTHER WORDS . . .

In a sense, cowardly people die many times during their
lifetimes. But the brave experience death only once.

LEARNING HOW TO LIVE IS THE CENTRAL TEACHING OF ANY legitimate religion or philosophy. Since this is our only life — and a proving ground for the hereafter — how we live is crucial. Our life is like a play — a short-lived phenomenon with a beginning, middle, and end. Some acts in this drama are more pleasant than others, but living well means that we need to learn to embrace the whole production; we must learn how to live.

But learning how to *die* is also important. It requires putting our lives in proper perspective. When we're young, the idea of death seems as irrelevant to us as mortgages, taxes, health problems, and all the other boring issues adults complain about. Young people live in an ever-present *now* — something that is, was, and always will be, unchanging and limitless. As we get older, we realize that life is *all about* changes and limits. As John Henry Newman writes: "To live is to change, and to be perfect is to have changed often."

Death is the ultimate change. If we refuse to accept that death is final and unavoidable, we will become more fearful the nearer we get to our inevitable end. Growing in wisdom means overcoming this fear, seeing death as a friend we've heard about but never met. We need to understand and prepare for this friend during our lives so that when he arrives at last, we can welcome him with open arms.

I learned that courage was not the absence of fear, but the triumph over it. The brave man is not he who does not feel afraid, but he who conquers that fear.
NELSON MANDELA

54. SEEK OUT SILENCE.

When to the sessions of sweet silent thought
I summon up remembrance of things past . . .

SONNET 30

IN OTHER WORDS . . .

It is better to be criticized for being too quiet
than for talking too much.

EXTRAVERTS TYPICALLY DON'T APPRECIATE SILENCE. Introverts, on the other hand, see its advantages. So, too, do wise people. The world is full of distractions, noise, and useless chatter. Most of the time, people form their ideas unthinkingly, haphazardly and emotionally, rather than through quiet reflection. In this chaos, silence can be a powerful tool for nurturing wisdom. Seek it out. As Malcolm Muggeridge writes: "We need silence to be able to touch souls. The essential thing is not what we say, but what God says to us and through us." At the same time, our silence should be loving and attentive. Follow the lead of St. Ignatius, who writes: "Speak little, listen much."

> *Silence at the proper season is wisdom,*
> *and better than any speech.*
>
> PLUTARCH

55. GET ENOUGH SLEEP.

The innocent sleep,
Sleep that knits up the ravell'd sleeve of care,
The death of each day's life, sore labor's bath,
Balm of hurt minds, chief nourisher in life's feast.

MACBETH, Act 2, Scene 2

IN OTHER WORDS . . .

Gentle sleep soothes away our worries. Sleep puts each
day to rest, relieves the worker, and heals distressed minds.
It is the most nourishing course in life's feast.

ALL OF US GO THROUGH TIMES IN OUR LIVES WHEN WE IMAGINE that we don't need much sleep. Sleep can seem like it has little connection to our quality of life. It often feels like a waste of time, especially when we're young. But we're not perpetual motion machines. Our body and mind need to be rejuvenated through rest. Whether we're young or old, we're at our weakest when we're most exhausted. Don't underestimate the value of a restful sleep and a decent meal. When you feel vulnerable, depressed, or emotional, sometimes a good night's rest is all you need.

Fatigue makes cowards of us all.

VINCE LOMBARDI

56. EMBRACE SOLITUDE.

Leave me alone;
For I must think of that which company
Would not be friendly to.

HENRY VIII, Act 5, Scene 1

IN OTHER WORDS . . .

Leave me alone. It's hard for me to think
with people around me.

THERE IS A WORLD OF DIFFERENCE BETWEEN LONELINESS AND solitude. Loneliness implies an absence or loss. Solitude is neutral. The difference is in one's a state of mind. There is an art to being alone just as there is an art to being with other people. Neither should cause us any anxiety. In fact, solitude gives us the resources we need to interact productively with others. If we don't value it, the time we spend with other people may be tainted with neediness or even desperation. "Don't care so much about what you are to others," advises Montaigne. "Care what you are to yourself." Being alone without being lonely requires passionately embracing solitude. After all, we can't hide from ourselves. Whether you're a hermit or a glad-handing politician, you'll spend one hundred percent of your time with yourself. Make sure you're the kind of person you want to be around. Otherwise, your solitude will always be mere loneliness.

> *The greatest thing in the world*
> *is to know how to belong to oneself.*

MICHEL DE MONTAIGNE

57. DON'T JUST TRAVEL — EXPLORE.

Home-keeping youth have ever homely wits.
I rather would entreat thy company,
To see the wonder of the world abroad,
Than, living dully sluggardized at home,
Wear out thy youth with shapeless idleness.

TWO GENTLEMEN OF VERONA, Act 1, Scene 1

IN OTHER WORDS . . .

Young homebodies always have commonplace minds.
Join me to see the distant wonders of the world rather than
wasting your youth living aimlessly as a sluggard at home.

THE MOST SATISFYING MOMENTS AS A TRAVELER RARELY TAKE place in museums or resorts. They occur when we meet local inhabitants on their own terms and in their own settings; when we learn what they think is unique about their families, homes, and towns. When we travel, let us seek out extraordinary people in ordinary places. Trips become adventures only when we step outside the neat circle of sights and activities curated for tourists. Then, when we return to our native land, we have fresh eyes and a richer understanding of the world. The true purpose of this kind of travel isn't relaxation or knowledge, but *wisdom*. "We shall not cease from exploration," writes T. S. Eliot. "And the end of all our exploring will be to arrive where we started and know the place for the first time." Don't travel to see but to understand.

*The whole object of travel is not to set foot on foreign land;
it is at last to set foot on one's own country as a foreign land.*

G. K. CHESTERTON

58. DON'T SURRENDER TO LESSER VERSIONS OF YOURSELF.

This above all: to thine own self be true.
And it must follow, as the night the day,
Thou canst not then be false to any man.

HAMLET, Act 1, Scene 3

IN OTHER WORDS . . .

Above all, be true to yourself. If you are, it follows
that you can't be false to anyone.

"KNOW THYSELF" IS THE FIRST COMMANDMENT OF WISDOM. Without it, all other virtues are at risk. Our process of self-discovery begins in childhood and continues well into adulthood. However, we should already have made certain discoveries: the importance of a strong character; doing the right thing even when it's difficult; placing others ahead of yourself; being honest; working hard; having faith in God. We should protect these fundamental truths with all our body, mind, and soul. No one can take them from us, but they can be lost or given away if we're not careful. The words of Ophelia are both a promise and a warning: "Lord, we know what we are, but know not what we may be." Stay true to your ideals so that you remain a person you can respect and love. And compare yourself only to earlier versions of yourself. All other comparisons are pointless.

> *To be what we are, and to become what we are*
> *capable of becoming, is the only end in life.*
>
> ROBERT LOUIS STEVENSON

59.
WORK HARD, BUT DON'T MAKE WORK YOUR MAIN SOURCE OF MEANING AND JOY.

Some kinds of baseness
Are nobly undergone and most poor matters
Point to rich ends. This my mean task
Would be as heavy to me as odious, but
The mistress which I serve quickens what's dead
And makes my labors pleasures.

THE TEMPEST, Act 3, Scene 1

IN OTHER WORDS . . .

Certain types of lowly toil are done for noble reasons. For instance, this humble work would be boring and awful to me, except that she for whom I do it makes it enjoyable.

WORKING HARD IS A VIRTUE. IF WE WANT TO ACHIEVE SUCCESS and build a legacy, it's critical. Laboring in a chosen profession endows our lives with purpose and meaning. It allows us to provide for ourselves and our families. But we shouldn't let what we do for a living define us. Our work will often not fulfill us creatively, spiritually, or intellectually. Ultimately, work is a means to an end. It allows us to pursue the things in life that matter most to us: faith, family, friends, service, and so on. If we make work our all-consuming passion, or if we base our self-worth on how much money we make, we'll likely be disappointed. In choosing a profession, try to strike a balance between your desire for meaning and your need for income.

> *Far and away the best prize that life has to offer*
> *is the chance to work hard at work worth doing.*

> THEODORE ROOSEVELT

60. Don't waste your time by worrying.

Care is no cure, but rather corrosive,
For things that are not to be remedied.

HENRY VI, PART I, Act 3, Scene 3

IN OTHER WORDS . . .

Worrying doesn't help but is actually harmful when it comes
to situations over which we have no control.

WE SPEND MUCH OF OUR LIVES WORRYING. WE WORRY ABOUT things we don't have and achievements we'll never earn. We worry about people we love and those we hate. We worry about our looks and our intellect. We even worry that we worry too much. We need to let go of this anxiety as quickly as possible. We shouldn't overlook obligations or challenges, but we must not let them control us emotionally. Nothing is made better by worrying about it. If we remain wise, anxiety won't have any power over us. In the end, we often don't even know what's good for us, so why should we agonize when our plans don't always work out the way we hope? Instead, let's take time to reflect on what we've been given and how fortunate we are to be alive. Stay wise, stay happy.

What else does anxiety about the future bring you
but sorrow upon sorrow?

THOMAS À KEMPIS

BOOKS TO MAKE YOU WISER

❖   ❖   ❖   ❖   ❖   ❖

The Abolition of Man, C. S. Lewis
The Aeneid, Virgil
Aesop's Fables, Aesop
The Analects, Confucius
Animal Farm, George Orwell
The Art of War, Sun Tzu
Basic Economics, Thomas Sowell
Basic Works of Aristotle
The Bible, (New Revised Standard Version, KJV, or other)
The Blank Slate, Steven Pinker
Blink, Malcolm Gladwell
The Book of Virtues, William J. Bennett (ed.)
A Brave New World, Aldous Huxley
Brideshead Revisited, Evelyn Waugh
The Bridge of San Luis Rey, Thornton Wilder
The Brothers Karamazov, Fyodor Dostoyevsky
The Closing of the American Mind, Allan Bloom
The Collected Works of W. B. Yeats
The Complete Poems and Plays, T. S. Eliot
The Complete Works of William Shakespeare
Confessions, St. Augustine
A Conflict of Visions, Thomas Sowell
Crisis of a House Divided, Harry V. Jaffa
Darkness at Noon, Arthur Koestler
D'Aulaires' Book of Greek Myths, Ingri and Edgar D'Aulaire

The Death of Ivan Ilyich and Other Stories, Leo Tolstoy
Democracy in America, Alexis de Tocqueville
Dictionary of Saints, John J. Delaney
Discourses, Epictetus
The Divine Comedy: Inferno, Purgatorio, Paradiso, Dante Alighieri
Does God Exist? Hans Küng
Don Quixote, Miguel de Cervantes
Eichmann in Jerusalem, Hannah Arendt
An Essay Concerning Human Understanding, John Locke
Faust, Johann Wolfgang von Goethe
The Federalist Papers, A. Hamilton, J. Madison, J. Jay
Freakonomics, Steven Levitt and Stephen Dubner
The Fountainhead, Ayn Rand
Free to Choose, Milton and Rose Friedman
Gulag Archipelago, Alexander Solzhenitsyn
Guns, Germs, and Steel, Jared Diamond
Hamilton, Ron Chernow
Handbook of Christian Apologetics, Peter Kreeft, Ronald Tacelli
The Heart of Darkness, Joseph Conrad
How to Live: A Life of Montaigne, Sarah Bakewell
Huckleberry Finn, Mark Twain
Ideas and Opinions, Albert Einstein
Hiroshima, John Hersey
Invisible Man, Ralph Ellison
The Iliad, Homer
A Kierkegaard Anthology, Robert Bretall (ed.)
Leviathan, Thomas Hobbes
The Lion, the Witch, and the Wardrobe, C. S. Lewis
The Lord of the Rings trilogy, J. R.R. Tolkien

The MacIntyre Reader, Alasdair MacIntyre
Meditations, Marcus Aurelius
Modern Times, Paul Johnson
Essays, Michel de Montaigne
Narrative of the Life of Frederick Douglass, Frederick Douglass
Natural Right and History, Leo Strauss
Night, Elie Wiesel
Nineteen Eighty-Four, George Orwell
Notes from the Underground, Fyodor Dostoyevsky
The Odyssey, Homer
On Liberty, John Stuart Mill
One Day in the Life of Ivan Denisovich, Alexander Solzhenitsyn
Orthodoxy, G. K. Chesterton
The Oxford Book of American Poetry, David Lehman (ed.)
The Oxford Book of English Verse, Christopher Ricks (ed.)
Pensées, Blaise Pascal
Personal Writings: Ignatius of Loyola
The Political Ideas of St. Thomas Aquinas, (Hafner Edition)
The Power and the Glory, Graham Greene
Praise of Folly, Desiderius Erasmus
The Prince, Niccolò Machiavelli
Reflections on the Revolution in France, Edmund Burke
The Republic and Other Works, Plato
The Righteous Mind, Jonathan Haidt
The Road Less Traveled, Scott Peck
The Road to Serfdom, Friedrich Hayek
The Seven Storey Mountain, Thomas Merton
The Seven Habits of Highly Effective People, Stephen R. Covey
Shakespeare: Invention of the Human, Harold Bloom

Sherlock Holmes, Arthur Conan Doyle
The Spirit of Democratic Capitalism, Michael Novak
Tattoos on the Heart, Gregory Boyle
A Third Testament, Malcolm Muggeridge
To Kill a Mockingbird, Harper Lee
Thinking Shakespeare, Barry Edelstein
Unbroken, Laura Hillenbrand
Utopia, Thomas More
The Vision of the Anointed, Thomas Sowell
The Wealth of Nations, Adam Smith
When Breath Becomes Air, Paul Kalanithi

_____

_____

_____

_____

_____

FILMS TO MAKE YOU WISER

❀   ❀   ❀   ❀   ❀   ❀

Acting Shakespeare (1982)
The African Queen
Amadeus
Apollo 13
Babette's Feast
Becket
Ben-Hur
Big Fish
Blue (1993)
Braveheart
Casablanca
Chimes at Midnight
The Chronicles of Narnia (2005–2010)
Citizen Kane
Conspiracy (2001)
The Count of Monte Cristo (2002)
The Dark Knight
Darkest Hour
Forrest Gump
Gandhi
Gattaca
Gladiator
Gran Torino
The Godfather I & II
The Green Mile
Groundhog Day
Hamlet (1996)

Henry V (1989)
High Noon
The Hollow Crown (2012–2016)
It's a Wonderful Life
The Killing Fields
Lawrence of Arabia
The Lord of the Rings (2001–2003)
Life is Beautiful
A Man for All Seasons
The Man Who Shot Liberty Valance
Master and Commander: The Far Side of the World
The Matrix
The Mission
The Passion of the Christ
Ran
Rocky
Rushmore
Saving Private Ryan
Schindler's List
Shawshank Redemption
The Searchers
The Seven Samurai
Slumdog Millionaire
Spartacus
Star Wars: The Empire Strikes Back
Tender Mercies
To Kill a Mockingbird
300
2001: A Space Odyssey

_____

_____

_____

_____

Songs to Make You Wiser

❖ ❖ ❖ ❖ ❖ ❖

"What a Wonderful World," Louis Armstrong
"Here Comes the Sun," Beatles
"Let it Be," Beatles
"The Word," Beatles
"For Everyman," Jackson Browne
Late for the Sky (album), Jackson Browne
"Man in Black," Johnny Cash
"Fast Car," Tracy Chapman
"Tears in Heaven," Eric Clapton
"With Arms Wide Open," Creed
"Anna Begins," Counting Crows
"Lover's Cross," Jim Croce
"Southern Cross," Crosby Stills and Nash
"The Girl with the Flaxen Hair," Claude Debussey
"Brothers in Arms," Dire Straits
"Blowin' in the Wind," Bob Dylan
"Don't Think Twice, It's Alright," Bob Dylan
"Forever Young," Bob Dylan
"The Last Resort," Eagles
"Wonderful," Everclear
Diamonds on the Inside (album), Ben Harper
"Boulder to Birmingham," Emmylou Harris
"The Heart of the Matter," Don Henley
"My Thanksgiving," Don Henley
"Closer To Fine," Indigo Girls
"Vienna," Billy Joel
"High Cost of Living," Jamey Johnson

"Chase That Feeling," Kris Kristofferson
"Everybody's Free (To Wear Sunscreen)," Baz Luhrmann
"Full Force Gale," Van Morrison
"Hymns to the Silence," Van Morrison
Moondance (album), Van Morrison
"Breathe (in the air)," Pink Floyd
"Baker Street," Gerry Rafferty
"Everybody Hurts," R.E.M.
"You Can't Always Get What You Want," Rolling Stones
"Freewill," Rush
"Hearts and Bones," Paul Simon
"Wartime Prayers," Paul Simon
"America," Simon and Garfunkel
"The Boxer," Simon and Garfunkel
"The Sound of Silence," Simon and Garfunkel
"Windfall," Son Volt
"The River," Bruce Springsteen
"Father and Son," Cat Stevens
"Let Your Soul Be Your Pilot," Sting
"Three Wooden Crosses," Randy Travis
James Taylor: Greatest Hits 1 & 2 (album)
"To Live is to Fly," Townes Van Zandt
"I Still Haven't Found What I'm Looking For," U2
"Pride (In the Name of Love)," U2
"Hallelujah," Rufus Wainwright
"Ramblin' Man," Hank Williams
"These Days," 10,000 Maniacs

_____

_____

_____

FRIENDS OF THE BARD

❖ ❖ ❖ ❖ ❖ ❖

John Adams *(1735–1826)* — American lawyer, statesman, writer, and second President of the U.S.

Samuel Adams *(1722–1803)* — American statesman, political philosopher, and founder.

Dante Alighieri *(1265–1321)* — Italian poet and statesman

Aristotle *(384–322 B.C.)* — Greek philosopher

Marcus Aurelius *(384–322 B.C.)* — Roman emperor and philosopher

Francis Bacon *(1561–1626)* — English philosopher, statesman, scientist, jurist, and writer

Bible

    2 Corinthians, 9:6

    Ecclesiastes 1:9; 3:11

    Matthew 5:16

    Micah 6:8

    Proverbs 1:5; 17:22; 20:11

    John 2:24–25

    John 13:34–35

William Blake *(1757–1827)* — English poet, painter, and printmaker

Allan Bloom *(1930–1992)* — American philosopher, classicist, and academician

Harold Bloom *(B. 1930)* — American writer and critic

Martin Buber *(1878–1965)* — Austrian-Israeli philosopher and author

Edmund Burke (*1729–1797*) — Irish philosopher and statesman

Miguel de Cervantes (*1547–1616*) — Spanish novelist and dramatist

G. K. Chesterton (*1874–1936*) — English writer, philosopher, dramatist, journalist, orator

Winston Churchill (*1874–1965*) — English writer, statesman, and prime minister

Cicero (106–43 B.C.) — Roman politician and writer

Confucius (551–479 B.C.) — Teacher, editor, politician, philosopher

Calvin Coolidge (*1872–1933*) — Lawyer and 30th President of the United States

Stephen Covey (*1932–2012*) — American educator, author, businessman

Benjamin Disraeli (*1804–1881*) — English writer, statesman, and prime minister

Albert Einstein (*1879–1955*) — German-born American physicist

T. S. Eliot (*1888–1965*) — American-born English poet, writer, and critic

Ralph Waldo Emerson (*1803–1882*) — American essayist and poet

Desiderius Erasmus (*1466–1536*) — Dutch Christian humanist, Catholic priest, and academician

Erik Erickson (*1902–1994*) — German-born American psychologist and psychoanalyst

Oliver Goldsmith (*1728–1774*) — Irish novelist, playwright, and poet

Friedrich Hayek (*1899–1992*) — Austrian-English economist and philosopher

Eric Hoffer (*1898–1983*) — American moral and social philosopher

Victor Hugo (*1802–1885*) — French poet, novelist, and dramatist

Thomas Jefferson (*1743–1826*) — Third President of the United States, writer, and philosopher

Samuel Johnson (*1709–1784*) — English lexicographer, critic, and writer

Thomas à Kempis (*1380–1471*) — German-Dutch priest, writer, and theologian

Søren Kierkegaard (*1813–1855*) — Danish philosopher, theologian, poet, and social critic

Peter Kreeft (*B. 1937*) — American philosopher, professor, and writer

Harold Kushner (*B. 1935*) — American rabbi and writer

C. S. Lewis (*1898–1963*) — English writer, critic, and academician

Abraham Lincoln (*1809–1865*) — Sixteenth President of the United States, writer, and philosopher

John Locke (*1632–1704*) — English philosopher

Vince Lombardi (*1913–1970*) — American football player and coach

Thomas Babington Macaulay (*1800–1859*) — English historian and politician

Alasdair MacIntyre (*B. 1929*) — Scottish philosopher

Nelson Mandela (*1918–2013*) — South African politician and civil rights activist.

Thomas Merton (*1915–1968*) — American Catholic monk and writer

Michel de Montaigne (*1533–1592*) — French essayist and philosopher

Thomas More (*1478–1535*) — English saint, lawyer, philosopher, writer

Wolfgang Amadeus Mozart (*1756–1791*) — Austrian composer

Malcolm Muggeridge (*1903–1990*) — English journalist and satirist

John Muir (*1838–1914*) — American naturalist and writer

John Henry Newman (*1801–1890*) — English Catholic priest, theologian, poet, and essayist

Blaise Pascal (*1623–1662*) — French mathematician, philosopher, and scientist

M. Scott Peck (*1936–2005*) — American psychiatrist and writer

William Penn (*1644–1718*) — English-American real estate entrepreneur, philosopher, and Quaker

Plato (*428–348 B.C.*) — Greek philosopher and writer

Plutarch (*46–122 A.D.*) — Greek philosopher and writer

Publilius Syrus (*95–43 B.C.*) — Latin writer

Theodore Roosevelt (*1858–1919*) — Writer and 26th President of the United States

Tom Robbins (*B. 1932*) — American novelist

Saints
    Augustine of Hippo (ROMAN, *354–430 A.D*)
    Anthony of Padua (PORTUGUESE, *1195–1231*)
    Francis of Assisi (ITALIAN, *1182–1226*)
    Francis de Sales (FRENCH, *1567–1622*)
    Ignatius of Loyola (SPANISH, *1491–1556*)
    John Paul II (POLISH, *1920–2005*)
    Teresa of Calcutta (ALBANIAN-IND., *1910–1997*)

Albert Schweitzer (*1875–1965*) — French theologian, writer, philosopher, and physician

William Shakespeare (*1564–1616*) — English dramatist and poet

Twelfth Night
Two Gentlemen of Verona
A Winter's Tale

Percy Bysshe Shelley (*1792–1822*) — English poet

Adam Smith (*1723–1790*) — Scottish economist, philosopher, and writer

Socrates (*470–399 B.C.*) — Greek philosopher

Alexander Solzhenitsyn (*1918–2008*) — Russian novelist, historian, and political activist

Baruch Spinoza (*1632–1677*) — Dutch philosopher

Charles Spurgeon (*1834–1890*) — American pastor and writer

Robert Louis Stevenson (*1850–1994*) — Scottish novelist, poet, and essayist

Tertullian (*155–220 A.D.*) — African Christian theologian and writer

Margaret Thatcher (*1925–2013*) — English stateswoman and prime minister

Arnold Toynbee (*1889–1975*) — English historian, philosopher, and professor

Mark Twain (*1835–1910*) — American writer and humorist

Oscar Wilde (*1854–1900*) — Irish poet and playwright

NOTES

Notes

Henry Jimenez

ROB CRISELL is a teacher, writer, actor, and attorney, but he prefers to think of himself as a full-time Shakespearean. He has appeared in many of the Bard's works, including the *Merchant of Venice*, *The Tempest*, *Hamlet*, *Macbeth*, *Much Ado about Nothing*, and *Romeo and Juliet*. He's the author of *The Zoo of Impossible Animals*, an action-adventure novel for preteens. He's also the author and performer of several one-man shows, including *Red, White, & Bard! A Celebration of Shakespeare in America* and *Hamlet's Guide to Happiness*. He's an instructor with Osher Lifelong Learning Institute. He teaches the Bard's works as a visiting artist in local schools. You can find his TED talk *How NOT to Hate Shakespeare* online. He is a graduate of Yale University and George Mason University School of Law. Rob lives in Southern California with his wife and their two kids. Contact him at robcrisell@yahoo.com.

CPSIA information can be obtained
at www.ICGtesting.com
Printed in the USA
FSHW010050070819
60755FS

9 780692 186732